United Nations

Linda Melvern

W

FRANKLIN WATTS
LONDON • SYDNEY

First published in 2001
by Franklin Watts
96 Leonard Street
London EC2A 4XD

Franklin Watts Australia
56 O'Riordan Street
Alexandria, Sydney
NSW 2015

Series editor: Anderley Moore
Designer: Simon Borrough
Picture research: Sue Mennell
Consultant: Ahmad Fawzi, Director,
United Nations Information Centre, London

A CIP catalogue record for this book is
available from the British Library.

ISBN   0 7496 3693 9
Dewey classification 341.23
Printed in Malaysia

Picture credits:
Cover: Panos: left (Howard Davies),
right above: (Giacomo Pirozzi);
United Nations: right below.
Inside: Corbis: 3 (Reuters/Chris Helgren),
22b (Reuters/Chris Helgren). Magnum
Photos: 1, 7 (David Seymour), 9 (Sergio
Larrain), 14t (Abbas), 14b (Luc Delahaye),
15 (Bruno Barbey), 20, 21 (Paul Lowe), 22t
(Bruno Barbey), 25b (David Seymour).
Panos Pictures: 5l (Crispin Hughes), 8r
(Howard Davies), 18 (Crispin Hughes), 19
(Paul Smith), 23 (Betty Press), 25t (Giacomo
Pirozzi), 27t (Jean-Léo Dugast). Rex Features:
11t (Sipa), 11b, 12t (Sipa), 12b (Sipa). Still
Pictures: 11 (Teit Hornbak), 2t (Mark Edwards),
2-3 (Gary Trotter), 5r (Teit Hornbak), 10
(Harmut Schwarzbach), 26 (Mark Edwards), 28r
(Jorgen Schytte), 28l (Mark Edwards), 29 (Gary
Trotter). Topham Picturepoint: 6, 17t, 17b
(Associated Press), 24, 27b. United Nations: 3br, 4, 8l
(UN photo 185265/A. Brizzi), 13 (UN photo
179194/Milton Grant), 16l (UN photo 18266/Fabrice
Ribere), 16r (UN/DPI/Milton Grant)

1. What is the United Nations?

The United Nations was created at the end of the Second World War (1939–45). When this terrible war was over, people everywhere were longing for a better world.

▼ The creation of the UN in 1945 was marked by a special ceremony in San Francisco to sign the Charter. Here, the British Ambassador signs the Charter.

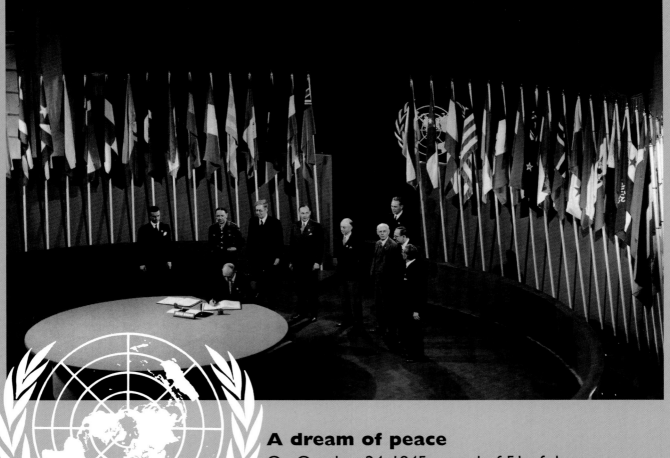

A dream of peace

On October 24, 1945, a total of 51 of the world's governments joined together to form the United Nations. They agreed to work together to try to make the world a more peaceful and prosperous place. There are now 189 countries who are members of the UN and have committed themselves to its aims.

▲ The official emblem of the UN shows a world map bordered by branches from an olive tree – a symbol of peace.

Aims and responsibilities

The aims of the UN are listed in the UN Charter. The Charter also states how these aims should be carried out, and outlines the responsibilities of UN members, their rights and their duties. In the Charter, the governments pledge to live together in peace as good neighbours.

Checklist

The aims of the UN are:

- to create a world free from war
- to bring justice and equality
- to help the poor people of the world
- to encourage friendly relations between states

▼ A UN peacekeeper helps people in Cambodia to return home following civil war. They had been staying in refugee camps in Thailand for safety.

▲ The UN helps those suffering as a result of war. Here it provides food for people in war-torn Rwanda.

Working together

The UN does not have any power over its member states. It relies on its members to follow the aims and the principles in the Charter and the decisions and guidelines adopted by the UN. Ultimately, it is up to each member government to decide if it wishes to cooperate.

Problem

Since the UN was created in 1945:

- over 30 million people have been killed in war, most of them unarmed civilians
- over 100 million people have fled their homes because of conflict
- governments have invested more money in preparing for war than in strengthening peace

The ideas behind the UN

Ever since it was created, the UN has tried to set basic standards for the whole world to follow. In 1948, it created a document called the Universal Declaration of Human Rights. This outlined the rights that the UN believes belongs to everyone in the world. These are your rights too.

▼ *This sculpture of a gun with a knot in the barrel symbolises the UN's dedication to peace. It stands at the entrance to the UN Secretariat building in New York.*

Spotlight

"All human beings are born free and equal in dignity and rights. They are endowed with reason and conscience and should act towards one another in a spirit of brotherhood."

Universal Declaration of Human Rights, Article One

What are our human rights?

The Universal Declaration of Human Rights declares that people have the right to life, freedom, and security. It states that people should be free from slavery, they should have the right to a fair trial, the right to marry and to own property and the right to believe in whatever religion they choose.

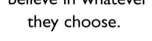

Denying rights

Although the Declaration was agreed in 1948, many governments still fail to give their people their rights. The UN tries to monitor any country which is breaking these rules through a special organization called the UN Commission on Human Rights. By doing this, the UN makes sure that the rest of the world is aware of each country's human rights record. This makes it harder for a country to get away with human rights abuses.

▼ *Eleanor Roosevelt talks to a colleague during a break from a UN meeting in 1951.*

✓ Checklist

The Universal Declaration of Human Rights states, among other things, that:

- everyone has the right to freedom of movement
- everyone has the right to work
- everyone has the right to equal pay for equal work
- everyone has the right to rest and leisure
- everyone has the right to education

● Spotlight

Eleanor Roosevelt, wife of US President F.D. Roosevelt, helped to write the Universal Declaration of Human Rights. She decided to do this following a visit to Germany after the Second World War. While there, she had seen for herself the destruction of war. The drafting of this document was the result of two years' work. It took a long time for all the states to agree on what the Declaration should say, but Eleanor Roosevelt was very persistent and in 1948 the Declaration was completed.

When Eleanor Roosevelt died in 1962 a US Statesman, Adlai Stevenson, said of her: *"She would rather light candles than curse the darkness, and her glow has warmed the world."*

2. How the UN works

✓ Checklist

The UN is made up of:
- the Secretariat
- the General Assembly
- the Security Council
- the Economic and Social Council
- the Trusteeship Council
- the International Court of Justice

◀ *An aerial view of the United Nations US headquarters (known as the Secretariat) in New York.*

The UN is divided into six parts. Each part has an important and different role to play in the UN system.

The Secretariat

There are people working for the UN in many parts of the world and there are UN offices in most countries. The headquarters of the UN, known as the Secretariat, is in New York. Over 8,700 staff, from all round the world, work there. They include economists, translators, secretaries, computer experts, security guards, librarians, lawyers, writers and journalists.

When someone works for the UN, he or she promises loyalty to the UN and may not seek or receive any orders from any government. The governments in their turn promise not to influence the staff of the UN in any way.

▲ *The entrance to the UN offices in Geneva — one of the three main regional offices of the Secretariat. The other two are in Vienna and Nairobi.*

✓ Checklist

The UN has six official languages: Arabic, Russian, Spanish, English, French and Chinese.

The General Assembly

The General Assembly is a big meeting at which every member state of the UN is represented. The General Assembly decides how the UN will spend its budget, and makes decisions on world issues. To make a decision or pass a resolution, two-thirds of the member states must vote in favour.

The General Debate

Once a year, all the members of the UN send representatives to the Secretariat for meetings to discuss any world crises and catastrophes. The main meeting is called the General Debate, and in this Debate, all member states can express their views on a wide range of issues. Most world leaders have addressed the General Debate of the General Assembly.

▲ Many world leaders have addressed the General Assembly in New York. Here, Cuban head of state Fidel Castro delivers a speech to UN member states in 1960.

 Problem

Each time the cost of the UN rises, the US share of this cost also increases. Some American politicians have argued that the UN is too expensive and they question why the US has to pay so much. Some of them have argued that the US contribution should be reduced. Meanwhile, the debt the US owes the UN increases all the time.

Who pays for the UN?

The costs of the United Nations are shared by its members. Each state pays a different amount. The founders of the United Nations decided that the world's rich countries should pay more for the UN than the world's poor countries. The US is the world's richest country and so it pays more than any other UN member. Many of the world's poorest countries, including Rwanda, Sierra Leone, Mauritania, Cambodia, St Kitts and Nevis, pay only a small amount towards the UN.

The Economic and Social Council

The UN's founders believed that reducing the amount of poverty in the world would help to create world peace. The Economic and Social Council was set up to co-ordinate all UN efforts to improve the standards of living of the world's poor. The UN works to try to bring full employment and create conditions of economic and social progress and development. As much as 70 per cent of the work of the UN system is devoted to accomplishing this task.

▼ A UN food aid mission delivers food parcels by plane during the UN-assisted Food Aid programme to help famine victims in the Sudan, 1994.

✓ Checklist

The 11 countries in the original trusteeship council, which now are all self-governing, were :

1 Togoland (under British administration)
2 Somaliland (under Italian administration)
3 Togoland (under French administration)
4 Cameroons (under French administration)
5 Cameroons (under British administration)
6 Tanganyika (under British administration)
7 Ruanda-Urundi (under Belgian administration)
8 Western Samoa (under New Zealand administration)
9 Nauru (under Australian administration)
10 New Guinea (under Australian administration)
11 Trust Territory of the Pacific Islands:
Federal States of Micronesia; Republic of the Marshall Islands; Commonwealth of the Northern Mariana Islands; Palau (under United States administration)

Trusteeship Council

The Trusteeship Council is not as important as it once was. It was created to look after eleven territories over which there was international control because no governement was in existence and for which members of the UN had assumed responsibility. The Trusteeship had to ensure that governments responsible for their administration helped the territories to prepare to govern themselves.

The International Court of Justice

The International Court of Justice at The Hague, the Netherlands, is the world's court. It hears cases in which one nation state blames another for wrongdoing. For example, in 1949 the UK took Norway to the International Court over fishing rights. The court ruled that Norway was within its rights to reserve certain fishing grounds for its own boats. International law applies to all countries. The court is not open to individual people. It is only open to governments. The UN General Assembly and the Security Council can ask the court for an opinion on any legal question.

Problem

In 1971, the court ruled that South Africa, a member state of the UN, must cease its occupation of the territory of Namibia and leave. South Africa did not abide by the court ruling, despite the UN Charter calling on each UN member to accept the decisions of this court.

◀ *The International Court of Justice at The Hague, the Netherlands.*

▼ *Judges of the United Nations' International Court of Justice.*

Spotlight

In 1979 the US embassy was seized in Tehran, Iran. Staff were taken hostage, and the US government appealed for their release at the United Nations International Court of Justice. Although the court found that Iran was violating international law, the hostages were held captive for many months.

Checklist

The court has the right to rule on:
- breaches in treaties and agreements between states
- questions of international law
- the interpretation of treaties
- the nature or extent of reparations to be made for breach of an international obligation

◀ *US Embassy employees are paraded blindfold before the world's press in Tehran, Iran, 1979.*

▼ *Iranian terrorists after seizing control of the US Embassy building in Tehran, Iran, 1979.*

3. The Security Council

The most powerful part of the UN is the Security Council – a meeting of representatives from 15 countries in the UN. The Security Council has responsibility for the world's international peace and security. All member states are bound by the UN Charter to obey the Council.

▼ *The first ever meeting of the Security Council held at summit level took place in January 1992. The world's leaders promised to co-operate with the UN in their efforts to maintain world peace.*

Permanent seats

Of the UN's 189 members, only fifteen are allowed to sit on the Security Council. Only five of those states are permanent members of the council. These five states are the countries who won the Second World War: China, the US, the UK, France and the Russian Federation. These five states have a veto in the council which means that they can stop any decision that they do not like.

Extra seats

Ten other states are represented on the Security Council. These are states which sit in the ten non-permanent positions, and they are chosen by the General Assembly. These states sit in the council for two years, then ten different states are chosen. The Presidency of the Security Council also changes – it is held by a different country each month.

Preventing war

When there are disagreements between states, first and foremost, it is the job of the Security Council to mediate between them – to try to help them to sort out any arguments before these arguments escalate into war.

If one country is being attacked by another country it can turn to the UN for help. There are then several things that the Security Council can do. The Security Council can try to stop UN members from trading with the aggressive country. It can send negotiators to help the countries to resolve their differences. The Council can forbid countries to sell arms to aggressive states. This is called an arms embargo.

Sometimes the Security Council gives the authority for states to take action. This was the case when Iraq invaded Kuwait in 1990. In this instance America led a group of states in military action to force Iraq to withdraw from Kuwait. This military coalition was agreed to by the Security Council.

▲ British troops involved in the liberation of Kuwait from Iraqi invasion, 1990.

▼ UN peacekeepers from France are seen guarding the airport in Sarajevo, Bosnia, during the civil war that followed the collapse of Yugoslavia in 1991.

A world police force

When the UN was created, the Council was to be the world police force, making sure all the states abided by international laws. The founders of the UN believed that in order to have a stable world, the Security Council must have the means to prevent conflict – with force if necessary.

▲ UN peacekeepers from Japan wearing the distinctive blue beret of their uniform disembark from their UN transport plane in Cambodia.

Time for reform?

The decision to have five permanent members on the Security Council was taken when the UN was created in 1945. However, the world has changed a great deal since then and the number of countries that are members of the UN has grown. Some argue that this should be reflected in the Security Council. It has been suggested, for example, that Germany and Japan should be allowed permanent seats because of their economic power, and there are claims from large-population countries, such as Brazil and India, to have more power in the UN. Discussions about changes to the Security Council have been taking place for some years with no agreement.

4. The Secretary General

The UN is headed by one person – the Secretary General. He or she must ensure that the UN operates efficiently and that the whole UN family is working well together and co-ordinating its activities. The Secretary General has to try to please all UN members and particularly the five most powerful states – the permanent members of the Security Council.

▲ Boutros Boutros-Ghali visits a UN-supported orphanage in Somalia in 1993, together with a commander of UN peacekeepers.

▶ Unlike previous Secretaries General, Kofi Annan was chosen from among the staff of the UN Secretariat where he had worked for 30 years.

The role of the Secretary General

In the eyes of the world, the Secretary General stands for the UN as a whole. The Secretary General is said to be a spokesperson for all humankind. The holder of this office must try to persuade the member states to uphold the ideals outlined in the Charter. This has been called the most impossible job in the world – although all UN members have signed the Charter, all states want to follow their own interests.

● Spotlight

In February 1998, Secretary General Kofi Annan went to Baghdad to meet with Iraq's leader, Saddam Hussein. Hussein was denying UN weapons inspectors access to sites where it was thought Iraq was manufacturing weapons of mass destruction. The UN Security Council was determined to prevent Iraq from making such terrible weapons; unless the inspectors were allowed in, certain members of the Security Council threatened to bomb Iraq. Annan's quiet diplomacy managed to persuade Hussein to let the inspectors back in.

▲ Kofi Annan meets Saddam Hussein in Baghdad in 1998 in an effort to persuade the Iraqi leader to allow UN weapons inspectors to assess the extent of Iraq's military strength.

The Secretary General has to warn the Security Council about any problems which might develop and which may threaten peace and security. The Secretary General has a duty to act as a mediator when conflict threatens; when member states are at loggerheads the Secretary General must do all he can in order to avoid conflict.

◀ Inspectors from the UN Special Commission, UNSCOM, in Baghdad, 1997. It was their job to ensure the elimination of Iraq's weapons of mass destruction.

5. UN peacekeepers

The main aim of the United Nations is to create a world free from war. Sometimes the only way to keep the peace is to have soldiers acting as a police force in a war zone to separate the two sides. The United Nations has soldiers for peace called peacekeepers.

What is peacekeeping?

Peacekeeping grew out of the need to have neutral soldiers standing between two enemies. After international politicians and UN negotiators have persuaded two enemies to come to an agreement, UN soldiers go into the area to make sure that the enemies obey the ceasefires and truces which have been negotiated.

Peacekeepers rely on persuasion and minimal force to defuse tensions and prevent fighting. It is dangerous work.

Peacekeeping today

UN peacekeepers also help countries recover from a war. Peacekeeping today is a combination of political, military and humanitarian action. Police officers, election observers, human rights monitors and other civilians (non-soldiers) go with soldiers into war zones as UN peacekeepers.

▼ *A multi-national group of UN peacekeepers prepare to destroy arms surrendered by warlords in Somalia.*

Peacekeepers sometimes help to get food to people who are starving and try to make sure that people have water that is clean. Peacekeepers can provide stability so that warring factions do not slide back into war. Sometimes UN peacekeepers watch elections to ensure that they are held fairly.

▼ *A UN peacekeeper from Italy gives sweets to children orphaned in the Mozambique civil war.*

✓ Checklist

- In Namibia UN peacekeepers helped the people to elect their own government and create a new and independent nation
- In Mozambique UN peacekeepers helped organize free and fair elections
- In El Salvador UN peacekeepers helped to reform a corrupt government and monitor the end of ten years of civil war
- In Guatemala the UN helped to establish a new human rights procedure to make sure people were no longer afraid because of violence and killing

The price of peace

Since 1948, there have been 51 peacekeeping operations. During this time, over 750,000 military and civilian police personnel have served in United Nations peacekeeping operations. More than 1,648 peacekeepers have died while supervising peace agreements, monitoring cease-fires, patrolling demilitarized zones, creating buffers between opposing forces and defusing local conflicts that risk wider war.

Volunteers

The UN does not have an army. For each peacekeeping mission, UN members voluntarily provide troops and equipment. Often, countries are not willing to provide their own soldiers and police if there are risks that there will be casualties. The peacekeeping operations are organized by the Secretary General and his staff.

▲ *UN peacekeepers from Egypt rescue a woman wounded during the shelling of the city of Sarajevo in Bosnia, 1994.*

In June 1991, war broke out in Yugoslavia. During the fighting, well over half a million people in Bosnia, one of the country's provinces that wanted independence, were driven from their homes or trapped in besieged cities. In February, 1992, the Security Council established the United Nations Protection Force (UNPROFOR) to create conditions of peace and security required for an overall settlement of the crisis. However, in reality, all UNPROFOR could do was protect relief convoys of lorries carrying humanitarian supplies as they went through road blocks and war zones to the citizens trapped in towns and villages.

Problem

Although the Security Council was confronted with a brutal civil war in Yugoslavia, some member states did not want to use force to stop the fighting. They did not want peacekeepers dragged into a messy military confrontation. Unable to fight, UNPROFOR was powerless to prevent the continuing violence against civilians and the frequent outbursts of fighting between factions.

The cost of peace

As the world has increasingly turned to the United Nations to deal with its conflicts, the cost of United Nations peacekeeping has risen. The annual cost of peacekeeping in 1995 amounted to approximately $3 billion. But governments around the world spend this much money every day preparing for war.

In 1994, the Secretary General informed the Security Council that peacekeeping commanders would need 35,000 troops to deter attacks on the "safe areas" in Bosnia-Herzegovina created by the Security Council. Member states authorised only 7,600 troops and took a year to provide them.

Problem

All member states are obliged to pay their share of the UN's peacekeeping costs under a formula that they themselves have agreed upon. But as of 31 May 2000, member states owed the UN more than $2.9 billion in peacekeeping payments.

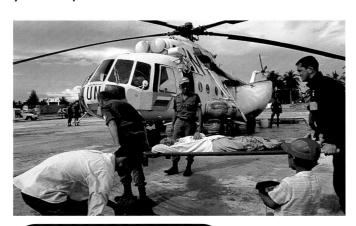

◀ In Cambodia an injured woman is evacuated by UN peacekeepers.

▼ In Sarajevo after shells have been fired at a UN base, a French engineer, part of a UN peacekeeping mission, runs towards a burning armoured personnel carrier.

Problem

Sometimes, the UN's member states fail to provide sufficient resources for peacekeeping. Peacekeepers have sometimes been handed daunting tasks by the Security Council – but have not been given the proper means to carry them out.

6. UN agencies

History shows us that prosperous people do not go to war. The UN founders therefore decided that the UN should alleviate the suffering of the world's poorest people. The UN tries to help poor countries to develop and to bring higher standards of living to their people. In order to do this, the UN has a range of specialised agencies and programmes.

The UN family

Each specialised UN agency or programme deals with a particular problem, for example famine, drought or world health. They are based all over the world to make it easy for countries to co-operate with each other in these vital areas.

UNESCO

UNESCO runs practical projects to raise educational standards throughout the world; it encourages countries to exchange knowledge and ideas about education, science and culture.

◀ A child in a school in Byumba, Rwanda, learns to write using a blackboard provided by UNESCO, the UN Educational, Scientific and Cultural Organization.

Checklist

Among the specialised agencies, funds, programmes and commissions in the United Nations family are:

- International Labour Organization (ILO)
- Food and Agriculture Organization (FAO)
- UN Educational, Scientific and Cultural Organization (UNESCO)
- International Bank for Reconstruction and Development (World Bank)
- International Monetary Fund (IMF)
- International Civil Aviation Organization (ICAO)
- Universal Postal Union, (UPU)
- International Tele-communications Union (ITU)
- World Meteorological Organization (WMO)
- International Maritime Organization (IMO)
- World Intellectual Property Organization (WIPO)
- World Health Organization (WHO)
- UN International Children's Emergency Fund (UNICEF)
- UN Environment Programme (UNEP)
- UN Development Programme (UNDP)
- UN High Commission for Refugees (UNHCR)
- UN Aids Programme (UNAIDS)

The World Bank

The World Bank receives money from member states – in proportion to their wealth and trade – and lends it to developing countries in order to help productive investment projects.

International Monetary Fund

The IMF promotes international monetary cooperation and helps ensure that there is monetary stability so that world trade can expand and grow. With economic growth come high levels of employment and improved standards of living. The fund also helps countries to pay debts during times of difficulty.

The World Health Organization

The World Health Organization aims to improve the standard of health throughout the world. It tries to help countries provide better health services for their people. It also tries to stop disease spreading from country to country. It supports research on the

▲ *Advertising used by the World Health Organization to increase public awareness of its work.*

prevention and control of disease and collects statistics on the state of the world's health. It funds health education programmes. When floods, famine, earthquakes and wars happen, there are WHO medical teams quickly on the spot to help.

UNICEF

The UN International Children's Emergency Fund was created in 1946 to provide help for all the children suffering because of the Second World War. There are still people who work for UNICEF throughout the world helping local communities to care for their children and to provide those who are in desperate need with health care, food, education and safe water. One vital problem is the increasing number of children worldwide – an estimated 300,000 children, some as young as eight – who are involved in 30 conflicts around the world as soldiers. UNICEF is trying to reintegrate some of these young soldiers back into the community.

UNICEF promotes the Convention on the Rights of the Child, an agreement which provides the rules for all countries on how to treat their children. Some of the rules include a child's right to life, the right to protection from harm, the right to the highest standards of health care, the right to free primary education.

▲ In Malawi a child is immunised at a health clinic.

◀ In Greece in 1949 this little boy tries on his first ever pair of shoes, given to him by UNICEF.

 Spotlight

In 1991 WHO and UNICEF announced the immunisation of 80 per cent of the developing world's young against major childhood killer diseases. These two agencies have carried out a world immunisation campaign against six killer diseases, saving the lives of more than 2 million children every year.

▲ UN agricultural specialists introduce improvements to food production on the Ivory Coast. Research takes place into the different varieties of rice to grow and the best irrigation methods to use.

The Food and Agriculture Organization

The FAO helps the poor countries of the world to improve their efficiency in food production. This specialised agency tries to ensure humanity's freedom from hunger. The work of the FAO is based on the old Chinese proverb: "Give a man a fish and he will eat for a day. Teach him to fish and he will eat for a lifetime." The FAO tries to teach people new methods of food production and how best to use the world's natural resources.

The UN Environment Programme

The UN Environment Programme was created in 1972 after a UN conference where 114 countries discussed the damage being done to the world by pollution. It was decided to set up a system to monitor what was happening, to encourage and coordinate policies for the reduction of pollution in all its various forms, and to carry out research.

▲ *In Bangkok, Thailand, those who work at the side of the street are advised to wear a mask because of the high levels of pollution in the air.*

What the UN Environment Programme does

In the past few years it has become increasingly obvious that the world's resources – water, fuel, land, clean air – are running out. The UN Environment Programme is trying to protect and improve these vital resources for everyone and to encourage the world's governments to take these problems more seriously.

▶ *The German Federal Chancellor Helmut Kohl addresses the UN Earth Summit in 1992. This was a landmark event during which governments discussed the most urgent environment problems.*

 Spotlight

Agenda 21

In 1992 an Earth Summit – the UN Conference on Environment and Development – was held in Rio de Janeiro, Brazil. At this meeting, Agenda 21 was adopted.

Agenda 21 is a blueprint for the development of the world with regard to the use of fresh water, forests, soil and fish stocks. This followed concern about the deteriorating global environment with rising levels of greenhouse gas emissions, toxic pollution and solid waste.

The governments at the Earth Summit agreed to make a stronger commitment to such issues and place the future of the planet at the forefront of their concerns. Many of the world's poor countries have argued that the rich countries use up most of the earth's resources and cause the most pollution.

Today, the UN's task of keeping the peace and trying to find solutions to international problems has been extended to include a wide-ranging number of roles. These include:

Gathering vital information

The UN system provides a useful statistical- and information-gathering centre, where information on all areas of human life vital to survival is collected and shared.

Actively helping the poor

The UN offers practical aid to the world's poor countries, helping their people to have clean water or training them to use agricultural tools such as tractors and seed-sowing equipment.

Tackling global issues

The UN system is increasingly pooling its efforts to tackle complex problems that defy the efforts of any country acting on its own. The Joint Programme on AIDS, for example, is made up of six agencies who are helping countries share information and expertise to try to combat an epidemic that has struck over 45 million people worldwide.

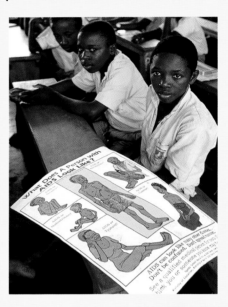

▶ *In Uganda, school children receive lessons about the disease Aids, and how best to avoid it.*

▼ *These people in Burkina Faso are being taught how to prevent their soil wasting away by the building of stone defences.*

Improving standards for everyone

The UN has been responsible for finding solutions to a number of important problems, for example by helping some of the world's poorest countries to develop agriculture or industry, working for women's rights, ensuring respect for human rights issues, protecting the environment, and helping countries to have good and caring governments.

The UN and the future

While the UN has not, so far, come close to fulfilling all the hopes and dreams of its founders, it remains the world's principal organization for the promotion of international peace and security.

Much of the world is insecure, unjust and dangerous, and in too many places its people are desperately poor. The achievement of the UN is that it is a foundation on which to build in trying to engineer change. Ultimately, it is up to each member government to decide if it wishes to co-operate in building on this foundation and create a useful and effective organization to try to secure a civilised future for all of the human race.

History has shown that it is not safe to leave world peace and justice in the hands of governments alone. We are all members of the world community, and we must all take our share of responsibility for creating the kind of world in which we would all wish to live.

▲ *In Mozambique, where the UN helped to end a civil war, a UN helicopter is watched from the ground by a young boy .*

Get involved

To learn more about the UN you can log on to the UN's website or contact the information centre in your country's capital city. By informing yourself about the work of the UN, you will already be starting to make the world a better place.

Glossary

alliance — an agreement between two or more countries to protect each other

arms embargo — an order to stop arms being sold to a particular country

besieged area — an area that is under military attack from which there is no escape

buffer zone — a term used for a strip of land that separates two military forces after fighting has stopped, sometimes monitored by UN forces

charter — a written contract, the term used for a formal and solemn treaty between states

civil war — a war in which two or more groups of people who live within a country fight each other

colonial rule — a country that is ruled by people from another country

demilitarised zones — a place in which no weapons, war materials or armed forces are allowed

developing countries — countries in which there is great poverty and a lack of the most basic requirements for the majority of people

disarmament — the reduction in possession of weapons

embargo — an order to stop trade

humanitarian — concerned with the welfare of fellow human beings through kindness

military coalition — one or more countries that decide to fight together against a common enemy

summit — an international meeting at which several heads of state are present

terrorist — a person who uses or favours violent and intimidating behaviour in order to persuade a government or community to take a certain course of action

veto — the right to reject a decision or action

weapons of mass destruction — nuclear, chemical and biological weapons that are capable of the indiscriminate killing of large numbers of people

UN headquarters

Public Inquiries Unit
United Nations
Room GA-58,
New York,
NY 10017
USA

United Nations in Geneva

Palais des Nations
1211 Geneva 10
Switzerland

United Nations Information Centre (UNIC), London

Millbank Tower (21st floor)
21-24 Millbank
London
SW1P 4HQ

United Nations web sites

United Nations home page www.un.org

UNIC, London unitednations.co.uk

UN office in Geneva home page www.unog.ch

UN International Court of Justice home page
www.icj-cij.org

General Assembly information www.un.org/ga

Further reading

1. *Basic Facts About the United Nations*
Published by the United Nations Department of
Public Information, 1998. ISBN 921100793

2. *Rescue Mission, Planet Earth*. A children's
edition of Agenda 21 by children of the world in
association with the United Nations with an
introduction by Boutros Boutros-Ghali.
Imprint London; New York: Kingfisher Books,
1994. ISBN 1856971759

3. *A World in Our Hands*. Written, illustrated and
edited by young people of the world, in honour
of the fiftieth anniversary of the United Nations.
Imprint Berkeley, California: Tricycle Press, 1995.
ISBN 1883672317

4. *The United Nations in Our Daily Lives*
Imprint New York: UN, 1998. ISBN 9211006546

5. *Pepito's Journey: a United Nations Study* by John
Travers Moore. Imprint New York: UN, 1987.
ISBN 9211003083

6. *Stand Up For Your Rights* by children from all
over the world. Editor Jean Trier. Imprint New
York: Two-Can Publishing, 2000. ISBN 1587284014

7. *What do we mean by Human Rights?* A series
of six titles. Imprint London: Franklin Watts,
1999.

8. *Sustainable Future*. A series of four titles.
Imprint London: Franklin Watts, 2000.